Enchanted Noel: Santa's Guide to A Perfect Holiday

FIONA BLISS

Published by FIONA BLISS, 2024.

While every precaution has been taken in the preparation of this book, the publisher assumes no responsibility for errors or omissions, or for damages resulting from the use of the information contained herein.

ENCHANTED NOEL: SANTA'S GUIDE TO A PERFECT HOLIDAY

First edition. November 10, 2024.

Copyright © 2024 FIONA BLISS.

ISBN: 979-8227912718

Written by FIONA BLISS.

Table of Contents

Enchanted Noel: Santa's Guide to A Perfect Holiday 1
INTRODUCTION 2
CHAPTER 1 | Creating Your Holiday Blueprint 5
Crafting a Holiday Schedule 8
Budgeting for Joy 11
Chapter 2 | Memories in the Making 14
Traditions Reimagined 17
DIY Projects for Heartfelt Gifts 20
Chapter 3 | Festive Atmosphere 23
Decorating with Intention 26
Crafting the Perfect Holiday Playlist 29
Chapter 4 | Culinary Delights 32
Signature Holiday Recipes 35
Hosting a Memorable Feast 38
Chapter 5 | Meaningful Connections 41
Cultivating Family Bonds 45
Spreading Kindness and Cheer 48
Chapter 6 | Reflecting and Recharging 52
Post-Holiday Check-In 55
Self-Care in the Festive Season 58

INTRODUCTION

Let's face it: the holiday season can frequently feel like a high-stakes juggling act, even while the smell of gingerbread fills the air, lights sparkle everywhere, and laughter reverberates throughout homes. Millions of families immerse themselves in the annual frenzy of celebrations, juggling customs, shopping, and get-togethers while fighting the clock. It's evident that the enchantment frequently gets lost in the turmoil, as 76% of families report feeling overburdened during this joyous time of year. However, what if things were different this year? What if the tension vanished, leaving behind the happiness, coziness, and camaraderie that genuinely characterize this magical season?

Welcome to a journey of transformation that will turn your vacation into something

remarkable. We're discussing how to thrive throughout the holidays, not simply how to get through them. Imagine an intentional, imaginative, and humorous holiday season as we set out on this journey. It's time to abandon the holiday hamster wheel and adopt a more rewarding strategy—one that unites families, spreads happiness, and gets everyone thinking back on the treasured moments made.

Imagine spending the eve of Christmas cozying up by the fire, drinking hot chocolate, with your house decked up in festive decorations, rather than rushing to do last-minute shopping. Your holiday memories are woven together when your loved ones congregate and share stories and laughs. With the correct resources and attitude, this dream can become a reality rather than merely a fiction.

According to statistics, 52% of people say that being organized over the holidays makes them feel more connected. Planning is more than just a tactic; it's the secret to opening the door to a more wonderful vacation. The holiday season is no longer merely a list of chores to complete, but rather a canvas for making

ENCHANTED NOEL: SANTA'S GUIDE TO A PERFECT HOLIDAY

treasured memories as people place a greater value on meaningful experiences than material presents. Families are spending an incredible 30% more on their vacations, focusing on meaningful moments rather than just gifts.

Only 34% of the billions who celebrate the holidays each year begin their preparations in advance. As a result, many families are hurrying through the season, lamenting the joy and connection they lost. It is understandable why 54% of adults express a want for a stress-free vacation. The good news? By looking for a guide that promises a new viewpoint, you're already ahead of the curve.

Imagine a holiday season that is full of deliberate decisions and happy occasions, where the spirit of generosity and community permeates every get-together. This guide serves as your road map, allowing you to learn the ins and outs of a well-planned holiday that isn't the result of chance but rather is the result of love, imagination, and happiness.

You'll find ways to reduce the stress that so frequently comes with this season as you read through these pages. You'll discover how to manage your finances effectively so that your festivities are facilitated rather than hampered. Investigate creative suggestions for customs that will appeal to your loved ones and help you create enduring bonds. With these doable ideas, you can transform every area of your house into a representation of the beauty and happiness that this season has to offer.

Not to mention the delicious food! Imagine entertaining your loved ones with delectable and simple-to-make festive dishes. You'll find delectable recipes that will become mainstays at your holiday get-togethers, transforming mealtimes into treasured time spent with one another.

How about extending kindness? In a society where the holidays can occasionally feel exclusive, we'll look at methods to support the community and encourage generosity and a sense of belonging. Beyond our own homes, the charm of the holidays permeates our communities, fostering relationships and generosity that make everyone feel better.

However, this book is about more than just preparing; it's about introspection and rejuvenation. We frequently find ourselves in need of a break after the hectic Christmas season. We'll look at ways to check in with our families and ourselves together, assessing what went well and what may be better for the upcoming year. It's important to remember to take care of yourself during the festivities. You'll discover how to put your health first, which will keep the holiday mood happy and satisfying for all.

Give up the idea that holidays have to be flawless as you enter into the upcoming chapters. Instead, enjoy the laughing, the small mishaps that become stories for years to come, and the lovely messiness of family life. The core of the holiday season is found in the relationships we build, the love we share, and the memories we make, not in perfect execution.

Your path to a magical vacation starts with each idea, tale, and tip. A glittering route that leads to meaningful events and enduring friendships replaces the chaos of the past. As the holidays draw near, you're not just getting ready for another round of celebrations this year; you're setting off on a pleasant journey and creating the experience of your dreams.

Come along with me as we change the way we celebrate. Together, let's combine creativity and tradition to create a Christmas tapestry that captures our identities as communities and families. The core of every shared experience, every embrace, every laugh, and every time spent together is where the season's enchantment lies, not only in the décor or presents.

Welcome to your one-stop resource for a magical vacation. Are you prepared to welcome the happiness, inspiration, and camaraderie that lie ahead? Together, we can transform this season into a festivity that will provide warmth and joy to you and your loved ones for years to come. This is where your ideal vacation journey begins!

CHAPTER 1
Creating Your Holiday Blueprint

WITH ITS FLURRY OF activities and expectations, the holiday season frequently surprises families by suddenly appearing like a cunning elf. The countdown to December starts abruptly, with a frenzy of baking, decorating, and buying that may easily devolve into mayhem. Creating a Christmas blueprint is crucial to controlling this festive rush because it transforms haphazard ideas into a well-thought-out plan that brings happiness instead of worry.

Examine the terrain for the forthcoming season beforehand. With paper and markers in hand, gather the family around the kitchen table and have a creative brainstorming session. Allow everyone to contribute their suggestions for customs, events, and festivities they would like to include this year. Involving the whole family creates the foundation for a wonderful holiday, from cookie decorating to relaxing movie evenings. Once the ideas start flowing, group them into categories, such as gifts, meals, and activities, and start picturing how these components will come together to form a fun puzzle.

A silent power that may make or ruin the Christmas cheer, budgeting frequently lingers in the background. The dreaded January credit card hangover can be avoided by creating a reasonable budget up front. To determine expenditure trends, compile last year's receipts, accounting for everything from gifts to decorations. Allocate funds to various categories, using experiences as presents and taking cost-cutting measures like potluck dinners or homemade gifts into account. Creating a budget encourages a sense of freedom in making deliberate decisions rather than restricting creativity.

Make a calendar outlining the celebrations for the season after the framework is complete. Consider the month of December as a tapestry, with every event contributing a vibrant thread to the overall design. Set aside enough time for preparation by marking important occasions, such as family get-togethers, holiday parties, and community activities. Remember to schedule downtime; even though the holidays are a time of great energy, setting aside time to unwind helps everyone refuel. Imagine relaxing afternoons while watching vintage holiday movies, drinking hot chocolate, and wearing pajamas.

A huge to-do list can be broken up into digestible chunks by assigning assignments deadlines. Assign deadlines to each of the manageable, minor steps that make up the planning process. For instance, instead of rushing at the last minute, gift purchasing can be made a weekly task that involves a few people at a time. Involving friends or family in a gift-wrapping party can be enjoyable and effective method to accomplish the chore while fostering a festive atmosphere.

Developing a holiday plan entails both order and spontaneity. Although a plan offers guidance, allowing for unforeseen events can result in enjoyable surprises. Joy can be sparked by impromptu trips to see holiday lights, unplanned get-togethers with neighbors, or simply attempting a new cuisine. The holiday season becomes a dance, with each step leading to amazing new experiences, thanks to this fusion of preparation and adaptability.

Examining customs that the family finds meaningful becomes a crucial component of the holiday plan. These customs create a special tapestry that captures the values and character of the family while also fostering a sense of connection and belonging. These customs, which can include a family game night, a special meal that celebrates ethnic heritage, or an annual ornament-making night, help to create a feeling of unity.

Another important factor is deciding what kind of environment to create throughout the holidays. Think about the emotions you wish to arouse in your house. A sense of belonging, warmth, and laughing are frequently at the top of the list. Cozy lighting, pleasant fragrances, and well-chosen décor can all contribute to this ambiance. Select decorations that express your individuality and feelings, such as handcrafted objects with a backstory or nostalgic appeal.

Making a holiday playlist may bring joy and vitality into the house. Every music evokes memories while igniting enthusiasm and delight. Make sure there is a soundtrack for every moment by selecting a variety of contemporary favorites and traditional carols. Conversations are punctuated by music, which also lends a mystical touch to the celebrations.

ENCHANTED NOEL: SANTA'S GUIDE TO A PERFECT HOLIDAY

As the blueprint develops, the value of community becomes apparent. The holiday experience is improved by interacting with the larger circle. These encounters, whether working at a nearby shelter, taking part in neighborhood activities, or just interacting with neighbors, give another dimension of coziness and meaning. Adopting a generous mindset spreads kindness and happiness outside of one's own family.

Involving children in the planning phase creates anticipation and enthusiasm for families with young children. They can assist with baking cookies, decorating, or even choosing presents for family members. Giving children the freedom to actively participate in planning the holiday experience fosters pride and a sense of responsibility while also producing enduring memories.

One way to create a holiday blueprint is to have mindfulness as the main focus throughout the season. The holiday mood can be maintained by pausing amid the chaos to enjoy the little things, such as the twinkling of lights or the laughter over a meal. Deepening ties and igniting meaningful conversations can be achieved by encouraging everyone to consider what the season means to them.

Making a Christmas plan during the rush turns the mayhem into a peaceful symphony of happiness and camaraderie. This considerate approach opens the door to a joyous season full of love and kindness. Every action, from planning and budgeting to interacting with loved ones and the community, helps create a magical and joyful holiday experience.

Every moment becomes a chance for connection when one revels in the journey rather than focusing just on the end goal. Families can have an unforgettable holiday experience that warms and delights hearts by embracing creativity, intention, and a sense of community. Planning carefully turns becomes a gift in and of itself at this joyous time of giving—an investment in making treasured memories that extend well beyond the holidays.

Crafting a Holiday Schedule

Creating a Christmas calendar is like arranging a joyful symphony, with each note adding to a season full of happiness and camaraderie. With countless chores and demands building up, chaos frequently reigns supreme around the holidays. Effective time management is essential to turning this chaos into a seamless celebration.

Evaluate your commitments first. Take a digital or paper calendar and write down all of the dates you know about, including family get-togethers, office parties, school functions, and community events. A visual representation of the season makes it easy to spot busy times and open slots, allowing you to fit in vacation activities without feeling overburdened. This is about striking a balance that permits both celebration and leisure, not just packing in as many events as possible.

As the calendar develops, give extra significance to events. Determine the things that are most important to you and your loved ones. Does the kids' academic achievement take center stage, or does the family have a longtime practice of caroling? Make certain times stand out on the schedule by designating them as non-negotiable. This method transforms the season from a list of chores to a compilation of cherished memories.

Create a cushion between commitments after that. Back-to-back events are frequently the result of the Christmas rush, which leaves little opportunity for spontaneity. A well-paced schedule guarantees that there is time to relax, enjoy, and be in the moment. Everyone's moods can be lifted by allowing a day off in between celebrations, which will further enhance the charm of the holidays.

Think about the skill of grouping related work into batches. This method works well for decorating sessions, baking marathons, and shopping excursions. Activities can be grouped to increase process efficiency and provide easier transitions between tasks. Choose a day and stick to it for your holiday shopping to avoid last-minute rushes that throw off the season's flow. When it comes to baking, why not make multiple batches of cookies at once? In addition to saving time, this offers a chance for family time in the kitchen.

Don't undervalue the significance of scheduling personal downtime. People are frequently tempted by the holiday season to cram themselves with activities, but relaxation is an essential component of a happy season. Make time for peaceful activities, such as reading a good book, taking a leisurely stroll to admire the decorations, or just enjoying a cup of chocolate while the snow falls. These little breaks improve general wellbeing and guarantee that everyone is happy during the festivities.

Include cooperative activities with friends and neighbors when creating the schedule. Holiday customs can foster a sense of community by extending beyond the family. Organize a cookie exchange or hold a potluck supper where everyone contributes their favorite food. These common experiences strengthen bonds and add to the season's richness.

When it comes to maintaining organization, technology can work in your favor. Think about using digital calendars or apps that remind you of things like tasks and events. Make to-do lists that correspond with your timetable so that nothing is overlooked. Digital tools may simplify the process and keep everyone on track, whether it's scheduling reminders for crucial dates or setting alerts for gift purchases.

Remember that the secret to a good holiday schedule is still flexibility. Plans can change as life happens. Unexpected events can become treasured memories by adopting an attitude that embraces spontaneity. Go with the flow if there's a chance for a pleasant adventure or last-minute get-together. Those spontaneous events frequently turn into the season's high points.

Include the family in the process of making plans. Everyone's enthusiasm for the impending celebrations and sense of ownership are increased when they are involved. Schedule a family gathering to talk about holiday preferences and generate ideas. By soliciting feedback, everyone feels appreciated, and the finished schedule captures the essence of the family.

Once the calendar is full, observe the general atmosphere. Remind everyone that connection, not perfection, is the aim. Think about changing or even eliminating an event from the schedule if it seems more like a chore than a fun activity. Making treasured memories rather than merely crossing things off a list is what the season is all about.

Regularly review the schedule. Take some time to consider what is and is not functioning well. This introspective exercise guarantees that the vacation will continue to be pleasurable. Adjust as necessary if particular tasks aren't working or if you start to feel tired. The objective is to create a flexible schedule that adapts to the family's demands while preserving the festive atmosphere.

Despite all of this preparation, don't forget to enjoy the small pleasures of the holidays. Think about the joy of family get-togethers, the glimmer of lights decorating the neighborhood, and the laughter shared over baking disasters. Instead of overshadowing these moments, let the calendar highlight them.

Creating a Christmas itinerary turns a hectic time of year into a fun adventure full of memories. Seize the chance to compose a song that honors the wonder of being with one another. The holiday season may unfurl like a beautifully wrapped gift—one that continues to spread happiness and love long after the decorations are put away—if careful preparation, adaptability, and a dash of imagination are applied.

Budgeting for Joy

While enthusiasm is in the air, a holiday budget frequently lurks in the background, silently waiting to be noticed. Every happy tinkling of bells is accompanied by the temptation to indulge in festive shopping. Having a plan in place is crucial to making enduring experiences without the financial shambles that frequently follow. Spending wisely can make the difference between enjoying a season of joy guilt-free and feeling overburdened by post-holiday debts.

Start by thinking back on previous holiday seasons. Examine what did and did not work. Did you feel satisfied with the lavish presents you received last year, or did you harbor a persistent sense of regret? Write down your ideas; this introspection lays the groundwork for creating a well-considered budget. Understanding your values will help you make decisions about how to spend your money. Making experiences a higher priority than material possessions frequently lead to stronger bonds and longer-lasting joy.

Make a worksheet for your budget. This might be as basic as a handwritten list or a spreadsheet. Sort it into four categories: experiences, food, decorations, and gifts. Limiting each category promotes flexibility while guaranteeing that no area is overlooked. To stay on top of things as the season progresses, include a column for estimated expenses and another for actual costs.

Including the entire family in budgeting conversations can provide unexpected results. Children frequently have distinct ideas about what makes the holidays joyful. Encourage them to come up with ideas for celebrations that don't go crazy. Perhaps more expensive customs can be replaced with a game night, cookie-baking party, or handmade gift exchange. Making decisions together improves relationships and makes budgeting a family activity.

Think about enforcing an adult "no-gift" rule. This refocuses attention on experiences while reducing the pressure to purchase. Plan a holiday activity, like going ice skating or to a local holiday market, in place of exchanging gifts. Instead of leaving with empty boxes and wrapping paper, this mentality change guarantees that everyone departs with memories and promotes connection.

Making wish lists for the younger family members might simplify gift-giving while controlling expenses. Urge them to put their desires first. This exercise fosters appreciation and teaches children the importance of giving with consideration. Share the children's lists with relatives and friends when they ask for present suggestions; this will assist to avoid misunderstandings and needless purchases.

Investigating do-it-yourself projects might give a unique touch without going over budget. The season is enhanced cozier and more charming with handmade ornaments, holiday sweets, and personalized cards. Organize craft sessions and make them enjoyable family events in which everyone participates. Any tangible gift is frequently outweighed by the ingenuity and fun that are exchanged during these times.

With a little imagination, eating can become a source of happiness rather than a financial burden. Accept potluck events in which each person contributes a dish to share. This method adds a range of flavors to the meal while also relieving the strain on one individual. Every family member can bring something unique to the table, resulting in a shared meal full of laughter and love.

Meal planning in advance helps avoid impulsive grocery store purchases. Provide a list of exciting recipes that use seasonal ingredients to save money. Saving money might also result from purchasing necessities in bulk. Keeping a well-stocked pantry ready for holiday cooking can be achieved by reducing impulsive purchases and last-minute visits by stocking up on non-perishables.

Despite their ability to establish the mood for the season, decorations are frequently very expensive. Embracing nature can be a cost-effective yet elegant approach to decorate your house. For festive displays, collect branches, pinecones, and other natural materials. Make sure that new décor doesn't have a price tag by hosting a decorating party where guests bring things from their homes to trade.

For a new style, think about reusing decorations from past years and combining different pieces. Old decorations can be given new life with a little imagination. Instead of expensive presents, consider making a do-it-yourself advent calendar and including small surprises or deeds of kindness into each day leading up to the holiday.

Another way to enjoy the season without going over budget is through local activities. Free or inexpensive events that are exciting and joyful are frequently featured at local markets, festivals, and parades. By fostering a sense of community and forming relationships, taking part in these events enhances the holiday experience. The delight of spending time together frequently overcomes the material costs, so check local listings for events in the region.

Finally, the generosity should not be limited to friends and family. Taking part in humanitarian endeavors cultivates appreciation and a feeling of direction. Take part in a toy donation program, plan a food drive, or volunteer at a nearby shelter. The season is made even more significant by these events, which serve as a reminder to all those engaged of the happiness that comes from giving back.

During the busy celebrations, frugal spending permits happiness without sacrificing quality. Every deliberate choice adds to a memorable and connection-rich experience. The holiday season may be a time of love, laughter, and quality time spent with others if it is planned carefully.

The relationships made, the jokes exchanged, and the memories made with one another are what make the holidays so magical. Embracing the spirit of the season without giving in to financial pressure is completely feasible. The holidays may be transformed into a joyful tapestry that doesn't have to cost a fortune if there is a clear budget, honest communication, and a little imagination.

Chapter 2
Memories in the Making

MOMENTS THAT CREATE a tapestry of treasured memories throughout the Christmas season take place amid the sparkling lights and the aroma of freshly baked cookies. The skill of creating those unique experiences that last long after the decorations are put away is covered in detail in this chapter. Every holiday is an opportunity for families to add their own vibrant hues of happiness, laughter, and camaraderie to the tapestry of their life.

Families move about, each with their own customs and rhythm. Everybody celebrates in a different way, and memories thrive in these variations. As the smallest family members try to reach the mixing bowl, baking together turns into an experience filled with giggles and flour-covered countertops. Cookie cutters may be used to create shapes like stars and trees, each of which represents a tale that is just waiting to be told, turning the basic task of rolling out dough into a joyful mess. Long after the cookies have been eaten, the smell of warm sweets and the sounds of laughing permeate the kitchen, transforming it into a lovely place that creates a lasting sensory experience.

Home décor frequently takes on a life of its own. From the attic, boxes of ornaments appear, each item containing a wealth of memories. The top of the tree might be crowned by an ancient, slightly crooked angel, reminding everyone of past holidays that were full of happiness and mistakes. Each ornament evokes nostalgia or humor, and stories about its origins start discussions. The house fills with more than simply decorations; it fills with emotion, history, and a sense of community that envelops everyone like a warm blanket.

Holiday game nights with the family can become the focal point of the celebrations. Cards and board games are scattered over the living room, and

ENCHANTED NOEL: SANTA'S GUIDE TO A PERFECT HOLIDAY

friendly rivalries are sparked by the resounding laughter. Both the spirit of competition and companionship flourish. These exchanges, which are full of lighthearted humor and the exhilaration of winning or the pain of losing, forge enduring relationships. The idea that these moments define the holiday spirit is further supported by the fact that, years later, everyone bursts out laughing when they remember that one game night when Aunt Betty unintentionally flipped the board.

Creating time for impromptu excursions enhances the holiday season's charm. Take in the stunning light displays as you drive around the neighborhood, where families are wrapped in blankets, drinking hot chocolate, and singing carols. As everyone enjoys the sights and sounds, each glittering house serves as a backdrop for stories spoken during the voyage, creating stronger bonds. These excursions develop into treasured customs that families look forward to each year, transcending their status as merely calendar occurrences.

Holiday celebrations can be revitalized by creating new customs. Perhaps the family embraces the vast outdoors and the thrill of choosing the ideal tree together by going on an annual hike to cut down the tree. As everyone trudges through snow or fresh fall leaves, excitedly discussing the virtues of each potential tree, the hunt turns into a humorous adventure. This journey produces more than just a tree; it forges a memory of companionship, with warmth and laughter adorning each limb.

The act of volunteering during the holidays adds a giving component that enhances the whole season. Serving food at a nearby shelter or planning a toy drive are two examples of activities that impart important values like empathy and community. When families band together to help others in need, they develop a feeling of purpose that strengthens their bonds. Telling tales of kindness and charity becomes ingrained in the family's story, giving the holiday season a meaning that transcends individual festivities.

Giving gifts may become an art form if you add personal touches to it. Personalized ornaments, homemade presents, or handwritten notes demonstrate consideration that goes beyond consumerism. An electric atmosphere that exudes love is created by the delight of witnessing a loved one's face light up at a thoughtfully prepared present. A cozy atmosphere that characterizes the holiday season is created by families spending these times together by the fireplace and sharing tales about the significance of each present.

Traditions can also be shaped by remembering people who are unable to join you throughout the holidays. The memory of departed loved ones can be preserved by lighting a candle for them or putting a place at the table in their honor. These actions turn sorrow into joy and serve as a reminder that family and love are not limited to the material world. As families negotiate the holiday season together, these experiences can serve as emotional pillars, firmly establishing them in love and common beliefs.

The holidays frequently turn into a flurry of activity, but it becomes crucial to prioritize spending quality time over attending as many events as possible. These times, whether they are spent making decorations in the afternoon, sharing stories over the fire, or just having a leisurely breakfast together, create bonds that last a lifetime. Everyone feels appreciated and valued when a hectic schedule is balanced with meaningful interactions, transforming passing moments into enduring memories.

It becomes essential to record these memories as families think back on their vacations. Throughout the season, gather pictures, comments, and decorations to compile into a family scrapbook. Everyone is reminded of the love, laughter, and adventures that were shared by this visual story, which acts as a time capsule of happiness. Looking through these scrapbooks in the future evokes sentimentality and coziness, reaffirming the core of what it means to celebrate with one another.

The holiday season creates a rich tapestry of memories that bind families together with each meal shared, game played, and story told. Every year presents a new chance to expand on prior experiences by adding new concepts and originality. Accept the beauty of imperfection; frequently, the most treasured memories emerge from those untidy times. The genuine spirit of the season is revealed in the laughing that breaks out when a baking project goes astray or in the delight of a loved one's unexpected visit.

Every Christmas season is a fresh start with many possibilities for happiness, creativity, and connection. Unplanned events, intentional customs, and routine encounters that take on remarkable dimensions when shared with loved ones are all ways that memories are created. Families may create a Christmas that is warm and loving that lasts long after the decorations are taken down by emphasizing the experiences that foster relationships. Memories created during this wonderful time of year will continue to shine brightly because the spirit of the season endures and is etched in the hearts of people who celebrate together.

Traditions Reimagined

Families are embraced by holiday traditions, which are a tapestry made of memories, laughter, and cherished rituals. But the ways we celebrate also change as life does. Reviving beloved customs not only pays tribute to the past but also produces new experiences that have a profound impact on everyone. Families can create moments that feel both familiar and thrilling through this technique, which combines sentiment and creativity in a delightful way.

Consider the time-honored customs of movie marathons, cookie decorating, and tree trimming. Although each adds a distinct flavor to the holidays, after years of the same old routine, these activities can get monotonous. The details are where the magic happens. Why not hold a unique decorating contest in instead of simple sugar cookies? Assemble a variety of toppings, such as edible glitter or crushed candies, and allow each family member to use their imagination. Give out entertaining rewards in categories like "Most Colorful" or "Most Creative," turning a straightforward exercise into an exciting contest that encourages creativity and laughter.

There are also ways to decorate trees in a novel way. Have a craft night where the family makes their own decorations instead than using the same ones every year. assemble your materials (paint, felt, beads) and discover your creative side. As a kind of memory capsule, each ornament narrates a tale of victories, mishaps, and laughter. Watch as the Christmas spirit blossoms in your home after hanging these one-of-a-kind pieces on the tree.

Remembering the power of storytelling is important. Ask family members to share their best holiday memories as you all assemble around the tree. This small gesture brings customs to life, fostering intergenerational relationships and inspiring participation from younger family members. Think about recording these tales in an annual holiday journal that is passed down from person to person. The notebook turns into a repository of common experiences that evokes nostalgia and laughter long after the season is over.

Traditions present a chance to be creative when it comes to food. Organize a themed potluck where each guest brings a dish that is influenced by their own experiences or cultural background. With cuisines from all around the world, the table becomes a lively buffet. Every morsel narrates a tale, strengthening your appreciation of your family's diversity. Together, develop a new recipe, transforming the process into an enjoyable cooking session that includes tasting and laughter.

Think about putting together a family holiday soundtrack that changes every year. Allow everyone to share their favorite holiday songs by combining traditional carols with modern tunes. The outcome? a music that allows for new memories while capturing the essence of each season. Play this playlist while you bake cookies, wrap presents, or just spend peaceful evenings by the fireplace. Music has a wonderful ability to improve the atmosphere and turn boring chores into happy occasions.

A little innovation in gift-giving can also be beneficial. Instead of concentrating only on material presents, think about planning a family "experience exchange" in which each member writes down a unique event they would like to share with another family member, such as a cooking class, a movie night, or a day trip. More than any material gift, the joy of sharing experiences strengthens bonds and produces enduring memories.

Volunteering as a family offers yet another lovely tradition to rethink. Select a nearby nonprofit or charity that shares your beliefs. Volunteer for a day at a community center, food bank, or animal shelter. Giving back together enhances the Christmas spirit and fosters compassion and thankfulness in all those participating. Additionally, these times strengthen relationships that last beyond the season and serve as a reminder of the happiness that comes from lending a helpful hand to others.

There's adventure out there, too. Make a family hike into a fun event as the weather cools. Prepare to go to a nearby park or nature walk, grab some hot cocoa, and bundle up. Take a leisurely stroll and take in the beauty of the season while searching for the best holiday light displays. In addition to providing a welcome diversion from the typical indoor activities, this shared experience strengthens relationships.

ENCHANTED NOEL: SANTA'S GUIDE TO A PERFECT HOLIDAY

A sentimental method to reinvent holiday customs is to make handmade presents. Plan a craft night where everyone makes gifts for one another. Consider homemade jams, personalized photo albums, or personalized candles. No store-bought product can match the unique touch that comes from spending time together during the creative process. Every present has a backstory and is a testament to the love and care that went into making it.

Holiday cards offer yet another opportunity to express your creativity. Consider creating personalized cards with inscriptions that capture the distinct personality of your family in instead of the typical printed ones. Add amusing family portraits or original illustrations. Write sincere notes that encapsulate your years' worth of experiences. By sending these cards out into the world, you may deepen the ties that bind your family together while simultaneously showing others how much you care.

As the holidays approach, consider new approaches to cherished customs that your family finds meaningful. Encourage candid discussions about the aspects of the holidays that each member values the most and how those aspects may change. A vivid celebration of love, laughter, and connection is created when you embrace spontaneity and welcome the unexpected. This trip creates a tapestry of the old and the new.

Every custom you adopt, modify, and reimagine adds a thread to the exquisite tapestry of your family's history. The holiday season becomes a lively festival full of love and significance when it is approached with imagination and purpose. Families may create a legacy that will inspire future generations by crafting a holiday season that resonates deeply through the joy of sharing experiences, creating memories, and building connections. As customs change, they encourage families to embrace the present and treasure the past while acknowledging the wonders of life together.

DIY Projects for Heartfelt Gifts

Making thoughtful presents adds a personal touch that store-bought goods frequently don't, making the Christmas season an unforgettable occasion. A handcrafted present is the most effective way to express your deep concern for someone. Let's explore a universe where sentimentality and creativity collide, encouraging you to create well-considered do-it-yourself crafts that have a special effect on the recipients.

Let's start with the traditional picture album. You can weave together moments that define relationships by selecting images of shared experiences from this rich trove of recollections. Gather pictures from important occasions, such as holidays, birthdays, and trips, and compile them into a lovely album. Include handwritten comments, doodling, or captions that convey your emotions. By reminding the recipient of treasured memories and your shared link, this personal touch raises the gift's worth

Think about making a customized recipe book for people who want to cook. Compile your favorite meals that you've shared or family recipes that have special importance. Include anecdotes about each recipe, such as the first time you tried a particular meal or a family get-together where it was served. To make a layout that is welcoming, use scrapbooking methods or bright pages. This gift preserves culinary traditions for future generations while also warming the heart and nourishing the body.

Candles are a great option for a sentimental do-it-yourself gift because they frequently represent coziness and warmth. Make your own candles with natural wax, aromatic oils, and ornamental jars. Choose fragrances that bring back memories, such as lavender for calm evenings or cinnamon for Christmas get-togethers. Add labels with inspirational sayings or the recipient's name to personalize the candles. These handcrafted items provide as a continual reminder of your considerate act while filling homes with wonderful scents.

ENCHANTED NOEL: SANTA'S GUIDE TO A PERFECT HOLIDAY

Customized mugs give for a personal touch while maintaining the charm of regular use. Invest in simple ceramic mugs and embellish them with ceramic paint or permanent markers. Compose sayings, jokes, or even basic illustrations that capture the essence of the recipient. After the design is finished, bake the mugs to solidify the paint and make sure they will hold up to frequent use. With every sip, these useful yet customized presents bring a little coziness to morning rituals and make people smile

A scarf made by someone skilled in knitting or crocheting is a classic present that envelops loved ones in coziness. To create a creation that feels as wonderful as it looks, choose comfortable, silky yarns in colors that complement the recipient's style. For a full outfit, think about including mittens or a matching hat. Even on the coldest days, this present reminds the recipient of your devotion by enveloping them in warmth and care. It embodies the spirit of love.

Hand-painted ornaments can be beautiful Christmas decorations for anyone with a creative spirit. Collect ornaments made of wood or clear glass, then let your creativity run wild. Create original designs that capture the essence of the recipient's personality using paint, glitter, or other embellishments. To create a memento that evokes memories of every holiday season, think about adding the year to the ornament. These decorations can be cherished family treasures that offer happiness every year.

Handcrafted bath bombs provide a little luxury and relaxation. Mix the essential oils, baking soda, and citric acid, then form the mixture into entertaining molds. Present these vibrant concoctions in jars or ornamental boxes with a label that lists the ingredients and usage guidelines. This considerate present invites the recipient to relax after a demanding day while indulging in the soothing aromas you've selected, promoting self-care.

You can express your creativity by creating a visual narrative through scrapbooking. Assemble materials such as stickers, patterned sheets, and embellishments, then start assembling a scrapbook that honors your partnership. Add pressed flowers, ticket stubs from events you've been together, or brief notes that contain inside jokes. This creative project shows the depth of your relationship by turning memories into real works of art.

Personalized calendars make thoughtful and useful presents. Create a calendar with pictures of your family or pictures that symbolize common interests. Put personalized comments or reminders on significant events, such anniversaries and birthdays. By adding a personal touch to ordinary life, this daily reminder of your tie enables the recipient to keep your connection with them throughout the year.

Crafting a little herb garden or potted plant becomes a thoughtful gift that keeps growing for anyone with a green thumb. Select a beautiful pot and fill it with dirt, seeds, or a tiny plant. Include a handwritten care manual that explains how to take good care of the plant. Every time the receiver takes care of their new green companion, this gift serves as a reminder of your generosity and represents development and care.

Another option to add affection to a present is to make your own skincare items. Make a batch of body butter, sugar scrub, or natural lip balm with basic ingredients. Present these in attractive jars with labels emphasizing the components and advantages. These items demonstrate the thought and work you've put into creating something unique while inviting recipients to treat themselves.

Making a meaningful do-it-yourself gift doesn't need a lot of skill; all you need is the desire to show love and consideration. Each project reflects your individuality and inventiveness, enabling the recipient to sense your connection. The holidays become more important since each handcrafted item conveys a memory, a narrative, and a piece of your heart.

Make use of these suggestions to celebrate the holiday season's creative and loving spirit. Every do-it-yourself project offers a chance to establish a memorable and intimate connection with loved ones. It all comes down to enjoying the act of giving and making sure that every gift has an impact that lasts beyond the holidays. Allow your emotions to inspire, your hands to create, and your gifts to convey the sincere relationships you value.

Chapter 3
Festive Atmosphere

The pleasant aroma of pine, twinkling lights placed along rooftops, and a happy Christmas song filling the air all combine to create a festive environment that brings warmth and joy into any home. It only takes imagination, planning, and a dash of holiday cheer to create this magical scene. A fairy godmother is not necessary.

The living room, the center of the house, should come first. This area frequently serves as the focal point of holiday get-togethers, where families congregate to laugh and make enduring memories. A towering, exquisitely decorated Christmas tree is studded with a variety of ornaments that narrate tales from previous years. Every ornament, whether it's a handcrafted item or a treasured present, evokes sentimentality and warmth. A delightful family activity that strengthens the bond with this treasured custom is stringing popcorn or cranberries together.

The ambiance is created by the lighting, which turns a plain space into a comfortable haven. Turn down the overhead lights and install a tapestry of warm, gentle illumination in its stead. While fairy lights, draped over windows or wrapped around banisters, create a mystical atmosphere, candles softly flicker, creating dancing shadows on the walls. The whimsical touch of stringing lights throughout the space lets everyone enjoy the subtle illumination that heightens the festive mood.

Next, consider the scents that permeate your house. Anyone can be transported to a festive paradise by the aroma of gingerbread buildings, freshly baked cookies, and simmering spices. Prepare classic dishes that encourage everyone to come together and partake in the culinary delight, filling the kitchen with the delightful aroma of nutmeg and cinnamon. Baking becomes more than just a chore; it becomes an event that fosters relationships via creative and humorous times spent together. Remember to include the children by having them assist roll out dough or decorate cookies with bright sprinkles. These pursuits turn into treasured memories in and of themselves.

The celebratory ambiance is further enhanced by creating a comfortable nook. Think of putting up a hot chocolate station with a variety of toppings, such as marshmallows, peppermint sticks, and whipped cream. Make sure there are cozy blankets and big cushions so that family and friends can cuddle and sip drinks together. In order to strengthen the ties that bind the family together, this nook can be the ideal location for storytelling, where everyone shares their favorite holiday stories.

Use considerate touches to embrace the giving spirit as the decorations come together. Gifts that are personalized offer a unique touch and show the passion and attention to detail that goes into each one. Gifts with handwritten messages attached convey sincere feelings and serve as a reminder to the receivers of the season's actual significance. A little ingenuity goes a long way; wrap presents in colorful paper, tie them with twine, and, for an added touch, attach a cinnamon stick or an evergreen sprig. Every package transforms into an artistic creation, ready to awe the senses.

The many customs that form throughout the holidays make a house seem like home, which is what makes the season so lovely. Think about organizing themed movie evenings when families may cuddle while watching their favorite Christmas movies. Establish a routine that permits relaxed evenings with popcorn and laughing while vintage films dance on the screen, bringing generations together in mutual delight.

The environment is brought to life by carefully selected decorations that capture the essence of the family's character and sense of style. Warmth and celebration are conveyed by every little detail, from garlands hanging along the chimney to wreaths gracing the entrance. Incorporating natural elements like pinecones, holly, and fresh greenery into the décor not only improves it but also ties the house to the splendor of winter.

Encourage family members to add their unique style to the décor so that it becomes a team effort that strengthens bonds. Everyone can express themselves through this involvement, which strengthens the ties that bind the family together. Every touch, whether it's making handcrafted decorations or setting up a special dinner table centerpiece, turns into a lovingly shared event.

ENCHANTED NOEL: SANTA'S GUIDE TO A PERFECT HOLIDAY

It is impossible to have a joyous mood without heartfelt music. Make every occasion a celebration by curating a playlist of folk songs, Christmas classics, and modern favorites. The appropriate music elevates the mood, providing a vibrant background for events or a calming setting for peaceful afternoons by the fire. No matter your level of ability, joining in on family songs brings fun and happiness to the season.

Don't forget to add a little magic to the house, maybe by giving family members little surprises. Everyone can be encouraged to enjoy the spirit of giving and receiving by receiving a surprise treat or a concealed letter here and there. The holiday season is woven with magic from these little moments.

Think about including deeds of kindness in the holiday plan as the celebrations progress. To spread joy outside of your house, encourage family members to perform community service. Volunteering at a nearby shelter or planning a gift drive are two examples of activities that strengthen ties with the community and teach important lessons about empathy and compassion. The warmth of the season is increased when the joy of giving is shared with others.

It takes an open heart and a readiness to accept the pleasures and messiness of the Christmas season to create a joyous atmosphere. Each sparkling light, delightful scent, and intimate moment adds to an experience that uplifts the soul and goes beyond the tangible.

Any home can become a wonderful haven full of love, laughter, and treasured memories when the spirit of the holidays is allowed to shine through. The beauty is in honoring the relationships made along the route as much as the celebrations. A treasured holiday tale that last long after the decorations are taken down is created from every hug, grin, and happy mayhem that are sewn into the fabric of the season.

Decorating with Intention

It takes a lot of heart, a little organization, and a little ingenuity to turn your house into a winter wonderland. The goal is to create a welcoming, cozy, and really joyful ambiance rather than overcrowding every available place with glittering decorations. With thoughtful decorating, every component has a function, adding to the season's overall vibe while letting your house shine without becoming overtaken by disorder.

Choose a color scheme that complements your style and the season to start. While cold blues and silvers can produce a calm, wintery atmosphere, traditional reds and greens add a classic touch. Pops of color combined with neutrals give it a contemporary feel. Selecting a unified color scheme facilitates the integration of decorations in various rooms of your house, guaranteeing a smooth transition between them.

Next, concentrate on a main idea. Setting a theme aid in selecting decorations that go well together, whether the venue is for an upscale party, a whimsical elf-inspired setting, or a rustic cabin atmosphere. The style of your wreaths, the ornaments you choose, or even the lighting you choose could all represent this. A clear theme gives your house a personal touch and makes it a distinctive way to show off your holiday joy.

No other element has the power to change the mood as lighting does. Replace harsh overhead lighting with warm, gentle tones that create a cozy atmosphere. A mystical glow can be produced by hanging fairy lights from mantels, hanging them from banisters, or even setting them within glass jars. An additional layer of warmth is added by using candles, whether real or LED. The aroma of pine or cinnamon mixed with the flicker of candlelight produces a warm and appealing atmosphere that welcomes visitors and makes your house feel comfortable.

ENCHANTED NOEL: SANTA'S GUIDE TO A PERFECT HOLIDAY

Adding layers to your embellishments gives your design depth. Start with bigger pieces, such as an eye-catching wreath on your front entrance or a gorgeously decorated tree. Build around these focus points from there. Garlands can be used to frame windows or to weave through stair railings. For a cozy touch, spread soft materials like throws and blankets over couches and chairs. Everyone is welcome to cuddle up and take in the beauty of the season thanks to these layers, which promote a tactile experience

Consider more than just the tree while choosing ornaments. To provide visual appeal, use different sizes and forms. For a more individualized touch, attach distinctive ornaments to gift wrapping, hang them from doorknobs, or arrange them in ornamental basins on tables. Think of taking a do-it-yourself approach and making personalized ornaments with the family to establish a unique custom that not only adorns your house but also strengthens bonds.

Adding natural components to your home gives it a refreshing genuineness. You might gather pinecones, holly springs, and evergreen branches and arrange them in bowls or vases. Use items like dried citrus or cinnamon sticks to fill your environment with the aroma of the season. These enhancements remind everyone of the coziness and warmth of the season while also enhancing your home's aesthetic appeal and fostering a sense of connection to the land.

Declutter before adding decorations to embrace the art of minimalism. A neat and orderly area is a blank canvas for your holiday décor. Spend some time removing anything that detracts from the attractiveness of the season. This highlights the attractiveness of the remaining holiday accents rather than depriving your house of its individuality. Every strand of lights and decoration should be able to shine without competing with the normal clutter.

Putting together themed vignettes all over your house encourages discovery and enjoyment. Place tiny groups of ornaments on shelves or side tables so that each arrangement can tell a unique tale. A dish of ornaments here, a few festive figurines there, or a warm scene with pine boughs and candles creates a story that draws viewers in. This heightens the visual interest and turns every area of your house into a little vacation adventure.

Don't forget to add your unique style to the décor. Stories can be told through antique items handed down through the centuries, handmade decorations, or family photos in festive frames. By establishing links, these objects allow friends and family to share in your memories. These unique touches, like a treasured ornament from your youth or a picture of a past holiday get-together, provide coziness and warmth to your house.

Adding festive fragrances to your décor scheme improves the mood beyond just the aesthetics. A sensory experience that enthralls guests can be created by simmering spices on the stove or utilizing essential oil diffusers laden with holiday-inspired fragrances, such as cinnamon, pine, or even freshly baked cookies. Scent has the ability to arouse fond memories and captivate everyone in the enchantment of the season.

Finally, when decorating, think about how your room flows. Choose a setup that promotes mobility and interaction. Make sure that visitors may move around spaces without feeling crowded or obstructed by decorations. Everyone can socialize, unwind, and take in the festive spirit thanks to its practicality, which improves the whole experience.

Creating an atmosphere that exudes happiness and camaraderie is more important than simply decorating your house to make it a winter wonderland. The craziness of the season can be subdued and a calm and welcoming atmosphere revealed by selecting a unified color scheme, developing a main theme, and carefully layering decorations. Lighting is important because it creates a cozy and inviting ambiance

A narrative that reverberates throughout your house can be created by embracing thematic vignettes, individual touches, and natural components. Every moment turns into a treasured memory as the aromas of the season permeate the air, beckoning loved ones to join together and celebrate. Making your house into a joyful retreat with purpose and imagination is a lovely trip that envelops everyone in the coziness and joy of the holidays.

Crafting the Perfect Holiday Playlist

A carefully chosen holiday soundtrack turns a joyous get-together into a treasured memory. Music is the lifeblood of festivities, establishing the mood and evoking feelings that elevate each second. It takes careful planning to create this aural backdrop, with each music contributing to the mood and capturing the essence of the season.

Start by thinking about the various emotions you wish to arouse during your festivities. From warmth and excitement to joy and nostalgia, the holidays evoke a variety of emotions. The correct music can enhance the occasion and foster a sense of community whether you're throwing a boisterous holiday party or a relaxed family meal. Making unique playlists for different events enables you to customize the soundtrack to precisely match the mood.

First, gather your favorite holiday music. Traditional carols have a strong emotional connection and bring back happy childhood memories. While lively songs like "Jingle Bell Rock" and "Frosty the Snowman" evoke a sense of playfulness, songs like "Silent Night" and "O Holy Night" instill a sense of solemnity. To create a varied selection that appeals to all ages and tastes, mix well-known favorites with more recent ones. The addition of modern musicians gives well-loved oldies new meanings, adding a contemporary touch that keeps the playlist interesting.

Incorporate festive music from other cultures to celebrate diversity. To extend the celebration, listen to songs that honor different customs, such as Kwanzaa and Hanukkah. Every song has its own tone and story, adding to the atmosphere and beckoning everyone to join in the celebration. A tapestry of sound reflecting the complex tapestry of the festive season is created by the blending of various influences.

Take into account the playlist's flow as well. As the celebration goes on, start with gentle tunes that greet guests and work your way up to more upbeat songs.

FIONA BLISS

This change promotes socializing and creates the ideal atmosphere for joyous exchanges. The excitement of the event is reflected in a well-paced playlist, which makes sure that joyful and humorous moments blend in perfectly with slower, more contemplative ones.

Choose music that improves the eating experience for the times when the food is being served. Conversations can develop without being overpowered by the pleasant mood created by soft instrumental music or delicate vocal harmonies. Mealtime may be made a special affair by adding warmth to the table with songs that conjure up visions of winter wonderlands or pleasant fireside conversations.

Don't undervalue the impact of sentimental music. Old songs frequently arouse deep feelings and recollections. Including songs that bring back memories of memorable times or the soundtrack of childhood into the playlist strengthens bonds between family members. Stories and laughter will flow as well-known songs fill the air, forming a shared story that enhances the celebration.

Additionally, interactive components can improve the experience. Think about adding a "family favorites" section to the playlist, where each member of the family shares their favorite holiday tune. Everyone is encouraged to join in and share their musical experiences thanks to this unique touch. This guarantees that everyone feels included in the joyous ambiance in addition to promoting a sense of belonging.

Make the most of streaming platforms. Numerous services provide pre-made holiday playlists with a blend of modern and old songs. Utilize them as a starting point, then add your family's favorites or lesser-known treasures that merit attention to make them uniquely yours. Because of its adaptability, the playlist can change and reflect the mood of each event, creating a dynamic experience.

Incorporate a few surprising songs to keep the playlist interesting. Surprise your guests with holiday-themed music from a variety of genres, such as hip-hop, jazz, or rock. Including a surprise element helps maintain the momentum and start conversations. Songs that combine contemporary beats with classic Christmas themes produce a distinctive atmosphere that appeals to a wide range of listeners.

Before the big day, test the playlist once it has taken shape. Listening through guarantees that the overall atmosphere fits your vision and that track transitions feel seamless. As necessary, modify the tempo and order to create a well-rounded experience. The soundscape can be finalized during this pre-event rehearsal, guaranteeing a pleasurable musical experience throughout the celebrations.

To keep the playlist interesting as the holidays draw near, think about upgrading it frequently. New songs that embody the spirit of the holidays and heartfelt ballads are released every year. Keeping up with new music gives you the opportunity to add lively tunes to your celebration. The excitement of finding a new favorite can liven up the occasion, enticing everyone to sway or sing along.

Engage your audience in the musical experience. During the event, invite them to perform their favorite songs, which could result in spontaneous dances or sing-alongs. Everyone is reminded that the holiday spirit lives in connection by this active engagement, which cultivates a sense of community and delight. As a catalyst, music dismantles boundaries and encourages recollections, stories, and laughing.

Making a holiday playlist is ultimately about creating an experience that speaks to love, laughter, and connection rather than just picking music. You can infuse your event with the spirit of the season by carefully selecting a musical backdrop. Long after the final song ends, the narrative that is created by each note and phrase is a celebration of unity. Allow the music to lead you as you get ready for the celebrations, bringing the warmth and joy of the holidays to every moment.

Chapter 4
Culinary Delights

DURING THE HOLIDAYS, when food takes center stage and turns ordinary moments into memorable feasts, the kitchen is a hive of activity. In order to create dinners that recall memories while embracing new sensations, families get together, each contributing a dash of innovation and tradition. Everyone is invited to gather and enjoy the delights of the season as the scents of roasted meats, simmering spices, and sweet treats fill the air.

Menus turn into canvases for artistic expression as the celebrations progress. Seize the chance to experiment with foods that speak to the history and culture of your family. Combine your favorite recipes that have been handed down over the years with some modern additions. The centerpiece of your dessert table can be Grandma's secret cookie recipe with a little twist, such as a dash of foreign spices or sea salt. The goal is to combine flavors in a way that tells a tale and takes everyone back to treasured memories with every bite.

The process of meal planning becomes a fun puzzle with perfectly fit parts. A well-rounded eating experience is ensured by arranging the main course, sides, and desserts into a unified menu. Roast turkey and glazed ham are examples of traditional favorites, but introducing a new dish can add interest. Imagine a colorful salad full of in-season fruits or roasted root vegetables dripping with honey. The table is visually spectacular and aesthetically pleasant due to its range of textures and hues.

The details are frequently where the magic happens. Think on the presentation of the food. The dining experience is improved by a well-set table with festive decorations and thoughtfully placed dishes. Make a centerpiece that embodies the season, such a bowl full of decorations or a group of softly flickering candles. Every component enhances the atmosphere, giving the dinner a unique and welcoming sense.

Baking creates a special kind of happiness and turns the kitchen into a creative and flavorful paradise. Cakes, pastries, and cookies serve as the backdrop for holiday cheer. Getting family members involved in the baking process creates a tradition of laughing and countertops covered in flour. Try decorating cookies so that everyone may show off their artistic side. Sharing the delight of making delectable delights makes it even more delightful.

Don't undervalue the significance of drinks. Drinks that uplift the occasion and warm the spirit are essential for holiday get-togethers. Adding hot chocolate bar stations with marshmallows, whipped cream, and peppermint sticks can be entertaining. Think of creating distinctive mocktails or drinks that capture the essence of the season. Toasting can be made much more enjoyable by serving a spiced apple cider or a cranberry spritzer, which can quickly become audience favorites.

Talk to visitors about the food they are eating while it is being served. By using storytelling to build connections, sharing the background of some dishes enhances the dining experience. In order to enhance the entire event with fun and cherished memories, invite attendees to share their culinary adventures and favorite foods.

Giving back is another opportunity that comes with the holiday season. Embrace the kindness that characterizes this season by cooking meals for people in need. Kindness and a sense of community can be promoted by planning a potluck gathering or making cookies for nearby shelters. Sharing food strengthens relationships and reaffirms that the spirit of the holidays is not limited to the house.

Holiday parties may involve special dietary requirements, so it's critical to provide a range of meals that suit everyone. Consider vegan versions of traditional dishes or gluten-free alternatives. When you experiment with options that appeal to all palates, creativity flourishes. To make sure that everyone feels included and content, roasted cauliflower can be a standout main course, and coconut milk can be used in place of heavy cream in desserts.

Frequently, leftovers offer a unique culinary experience. Making new recipes out of leftovers may be a fun task. What's left over after the Christmas feast can be given new life with turkey soup, casseroles, or even inventive sandwiches. This prolongs the celebration after the main event and reduces waste by allowing the flavors to linger.

As the holidays approach, keep in mind that food is more than simply nourishment—it's a symbol of joy, love, and connection. Food unites people, sparking conversation and fostering enduring memories. The kitchen becomes a creative center where customs flourish and new favorites are created.

During the holidays, the craft of cooking frequently transforms into a dance in which stories and flavors blend together. Savor every second of cooking and spending time with loved ones as you celebrate the process. Every meal tells a tale, every taste makes you happy, and every bite together strengthens your bonds as a family during this wonderful time of year.

Making a culinary experience for the holidays is a chance to use food to show love. Allow the kitchen to become a space where innovation and tradition collide, where recipes become treasured memories. Let the food serve as a mirror of the love, warmth, and laughter that characterize this magical season as the celebrations progress.

Signature Holiday Recipes

The kitchen is a flurry of activity and excitement amid the festive chaos of the holidays. With excitement lingering in the air like the aroma of freshly baked cookies, friends and family come together. As everyone joins together to create foods that evoke coziness and memories, culinary ingenuity takes center stage. Making delicious, sensory-pleasing meals and snacks turns into a treasured custom that enables everyone to show their love via food.

Let's start with the main attraction: holiday cookies. With dishes that involve little effort but offer maximum flavor, each bite-sized creation transports tasters to festive pleasure. A traditional recipe for gingerbread cookies that combines the warming flavors of ginger, nutmeg, and cinnamon beckons. A basic mixture of flour, sugar, molasses, and butter is used to make the dough. Spread it out and use festive cookie cutters to create happy shapes, such as glittering stars or jolly Santas. When baked until golden, they release a delicious aroma that entices family members and friends into the kitchen like moths to a flame.

It becomes an experience in and of itself to decorate these biscuits. Arrange a station for decorating with edible glitter, sprinkles, and colorful frosting. Friends and family may let their imaginations run wild and turn every cookie into a one-of-a-kind work of art. Long after the last cookie has been eaten, the memories created by the laughing and lighthearted competition over the most creative designs endure.

Now for the savory treats: a festive cheese board can add flair to any event. Every palate can be satisfied by choosing a range of cheeses, such as sharp cheddar, tangy goat cheese, and creamy brie. For a taste and color explosion, pair them with seasonal fruits like apple slices, figs, and pomegranate seeds. For texture, include a variety of nuts and olives, and don't forget the crackers! In addition to being aesthetically pleasing, this centerpiece encourages attendees to socialize and snack during the celebration.

Try a cozy holiday dish for something heartier. Any Christmas meal would benefit from the tasty and nourishing addition of a sweet potato and kale gratin. Arrange the fresh kale, thinly sliced sweet potatoes, and a thick, creamy sauce that has been flavored with herbs and garlic. Even the pickiest diners will be impressed when this dish comes out of the oven steaming and fragrant, topped with golden, crispy breadcrumbs. Serve it with roasted veggies for a vibrant, nutritious meal that highlights the abundance of the season.

Another popular dish for bigger parties is a traditional holiday ham. The ham's natural flavors are enhanced by the glossy finish created by glazing it with a mixture of brown sugar, mustard, and honey. Allow the glaze to caramelize and produce a sticky sweetness that will entice everyone to the table as you bake it gently. Serve the slices with homemade cranberry sauce to counterbalance the tartness and savory richness.

Without a dessert that steals the show, no Christmas table feels complete. With its silky filling and buttery crust, a rich chocolate pie is sure to turn heads at any event. Using premium chocolate is essential to making sure every bite melts in your tongue. Add a dash of sea salt and powdered sugar on top of the tart for a sophisticated touch that will wow your visitors.

Serve this rich dessert with a traditional eggnog to go with it. Eggs, cream, sugar, and a touch of nutmeg combine to make a delightful, creamy beverage that uplifts the spirit. For the adults, personalize it with a dash of bourbon or rum, adding a festive touch that lifts spirits. With a cinnamon stick and a nutmeg sprinkle on top, serve it warm or cold and watch it become the talk of the party.

A hot, comforting soup can enhance the intimate ambiance as the celebrations go. A heartwarming and delectable appetizer is roasted butternut squash soup, which combines sweet squash with earthy spices like cinnamon and ginger. For extra texture and taste, sprinkle roasted pumpkin seeds and a swirl of cream on top, and encourage everyone to enjoy every spoonful.

Don't undervalue the significance of festive drinks, even as food and treats take center stage. With its assortment of toppings, including whipped cream, marshmallows, crushed peppermint, and even a dash of flavoring syrups, a hot chocolate bar encourages indulgence and creativity. While enjoying the companionship of loved ones, guests can personalize their mugs and sip on thick, velvety hot chocolate.

ENCHANTED NOEL: SANTA'S GUIDE TO A PERFECT HOLIDAY

Finding methods to involve everyone in the culinary process adds even more specialness to the celebration. Sharing the effort makes meal preparation an engaging and fun activity, whether it's dividing up the cookie decorating duties or asking visitors to chop vegetables for the casserole. Children especially love being able to create, and their excitement infuses the kitchen with contagious energy.

Recipes for holidays can also be improved by experimenting with different flavors. With its acidic punch, a fresh and spicy cranberry orange relish can become a new favorite by counterbalancing the sweetness of pastries. All you need to do is combine fresh cranberries with orange zest and a little sugar to create a colorful sauce that goes well with savory foods.

Think of include a baking session where everyone may create delicacies to distribute to neighbors or community members in the spirit of giving. Making quantities of cookies, fudge, or other treats encourages giving and community, bringing happiness to people outside of one's own social group. Putting these snacks in pretty boxes or bags gives them a unique touch and makes sure the festive vibes are felt everywhere.

Every dish becomes a part of the Christmas tale as the day progresses and the table is laden with a variety of delectable delicacies. These recipes turn an ordinary get-together into a feast full of laughter, love, and enduring memories. Around the table, everyone congregates to share tales, laugh, and experience the happiness that comes from delicious food and wonderful people.

The kitchen continues to be a center of warmth and companionship as the celebrations come to an end and stomachs are full. Reminiscent of the happy times spent together, leftover goodies encourage impromptu get-togethers in the days ahead. Every meal captures the essence of the holiday season while fostering relationships that go well beyond the dinner table.

The essence of the holiday season is transformed from a celebration of food to one of love, creativity, and togetherness with each bite enjoyed. The memories made during these shared meals will endure throughout the new year, encouraging a sense of connectedness and thankfulness that endures long after the last crumb has been cleared away.

Hosting a Memorable Feast

Excitement is in the air as the holidays draw near, and preparations for get-togethers start to take shape. It takes more than just preparing a few dishes and setting the table to host a feast that people will remember. It involves planning an event that unites loved ones, makes everyone laugh, and produces priceless memories. Making sure that each visitor feels unique requires careful preparation and close attention to detail.

Start by selecting a theme that captures the essence of the season and your personal flair. This doesn't have to be ostentatious; consider something classy, whimsical, or comfortable. A clear theme establishes the mood for the entire event and directs choices about the meal, décor, and even the dress code. Warm lighting, rustic table settings, and nostalgic comfort food are all great ideas for a warm and inviting event. Choose elegant tableware, chic décor, and a menu that features gourmet meals if elegance is the goal.

After deciding on a theme, the guest list comes next. Think on who you want to invite, making sure to include some new people in addition to your family and close friends. The combination of the known and the unknown can enhance the experience and lead to fascinating discussions. To give guests enough time to clear their schedules, send out invites in advance, either digitally or on traditional cards.

Creating a theme-appropriate cuisine becomes the focal point of the event. To showcase the flavors of the season, use seasonal ingredients in your favorite dishes that your visitors will enjoy. Think of roasted meats, colorful salads, and decadent sweets to strike a balance between robust and light options. Add a few vegetarian or gluten-free recipes to suit different dietary requirements. Every guest may enjoy the meal worry-free because of this careful consideration, which guarantees that everyone feels included.

ENCHANTED NOEL: SANTA'S GUIDE TO A PERFECT HOLIDAY

The secret to a smooth encounter is preparation. Several weeks in advance, begin organizing the menu by creating a thorough shopping list that accounts for all of the ingredients required for each dish. Make a schedule for cooking and preparation as the feast day draws near. The last-minute rush that frequently results in stress is reduced when tasks are divided into manageable portions.

The kitchen is a hive of activity on the day of the event. The fragrances of roasted vegetables and spices permeate the air as meals in various states of completion are prepared, laying the groundwork for what lies ahead. Make cooking a team effort by enlisting family members or friends to help with the preparations. Let laughter fill the kitchen as you divide up the chores, whether it's slicing vegetables, setting the table, or making cocktails. By transforming the ordinary into joyful moments, this friendship strengthens the sense of community.

Establishing a friendly environment prepares the ground for a fun evening. Take note of the lighting and choose soft, warm solutions. An welcoming glow that promotes relaxation can be produced by candles, string lights, or a warm fireplace. Use seasonal decorations, like handcrafted place cards, colorful baubles, or evergreen sprigs, to decorate the table in keeping with the theme. A handwritten menu or a small gift for each visitor are examples of personal touches that offer a level of consideration that will be appreciated by all.

With a festive drink in hand and a warm grin, welcome guests as they arrive. The scene is set and mingling is encouraged with a signature drink, mulled wine, or a non-alcoholic choice. Make an appetizer spread so that guests may snack and catch up while the main course simmers and bakes. A lovely start to the evening is provided by a variety of cheeses, charcuterie, and seasonal fruits, which fill the room with enticing flavors and scents.

As the evening progresses, timing becomes increasingly important. Make a happy announcement and bring everyone to the table as the main course is almost finished. Make a toast that captures the essence of the occasion by expressing gratitude for the meal, the people, and the memories being made. The act of assembling around the table invites everyone to share in the moment and epitomizes connectedness.

Encourage conversation by including interesting themes once the feast has started. Reminisce about family customs, tell amusing tales from previous holidays, or talk about this year's fresh discoveries. The goal is to create an environment where people laugh as much as they drink wine. Feel free to add games or activities as the courses go along to keep the spirits upbeat and encourage attendees to join in on some lighthearted fun.

The dessert is the evening's grand conclusion. Whether it's a pie, cake, or selection of Christmas cookies, a nicely arranged sweet treat adds a gratifying finish to the dinner. Serve coffee or tea with dessert to entice guests to stay a bit longer and enjoy the flavors while laughing and telling stories.

Finally, thank the guests for coming as the evening comes to an end and they start to leave. A sincere "thank you" strengthens the bonds formed during the event and creates a lasting impression. Think about giving them a tiny memento to show your gratitude, such a holiday ornament, a handwritten letter, or a leftover goodie. By reminding everyone of the delight spent together, these considerate actions prolong the evening's warmth.

Putting together a feast that people will remember is an art form that combines imagination, forethought, and passion. By creating an atmosphere that emphasizes happiness, connection, and delicious food, the holiday get-together becomes a celebration that lasts long after the last course is gone. Families and friends will look forward to the event year after year as it becomes a treasured memory thanks to meticulous planning and a focus on coziness and warmth.

Chapter 5
Meaningful Connections

IN THE MIDDLE OF THE Christmas season's hustle and bustle, the relationships we create with one another frequently form the core of the festivities. Whether with family, friends, neighbors, or even complete strangers, this time of year offers a special chance to strengthen bonds. Concentrating on these deep connections becomes crucial, turning the hustle into something that has a deeper significance.

The spirit of the season is spending time with loved ones. Communities plan events that unify people, families congregate around dinner tables, and friends get together for comfortable get-togethers. Warmth, joy, and love are fostered by these times, weaving a web of shared memories that endures long after the holiday lights have gone out. The entire ambiance can be changed by approaching these events as chances for connection rather than as a set of duties.

Think of having a Christmas potluck where each person brings their favorite food to share. Every dish at this get-together serves as a platform for the sharing of customs and memories, reflecting the diverse backgrounds and histories of the participants. Free-flowing conversations create laughter and bridge generational divides. Simple things like exchanging recipes or remembering holiday celebrations from childhood strengthen ties and foster a feeling of community.

Creating original customs can strengthen family ties. These activities, whether it's making handcrafted ornaments or reading holiday stories together every night, create treasured memories that deepen family bonds. Every tradition conveys values and ideas from one generation to the next while telling a tale. While adults enjoy reliving their own childhood memories, children learn the value of being together.

During the holidays, giving back is also essential to developing deep ties. Whether it's volunteering, giving to neighborhood charity, or just lending a hand to a neighbor, doing good deeds spreads goodwill. Empathy and a sense of purpose are fostered when a family or community comes together to support people in need. These encounters remind everyone of the genuine essence of the season and bring people together in a common goal.

In order to foster relationships, communication becomes essential. Relationships can be strengthened and distances bridged with a simple phone call or handwritten message, especially when the other person lives far away. In addition to making someone's day, sending holiday cards with heartfelt notes helps them feel appreciated and remembered. Relationships that may have waned over time can be revived and touching conversations can result from small actions.

Making time for meaningful talks during this hectic time of year can have a profound impact. Provide opportunities for family members and friends to get together, talk, and express gratitude. These discussions offer a forum for introspection, humor, and emotional support. Everyone may communicate what the holidays mean to them when they have a quiet moment during the celebrations to connect on a deeper level.

Developing deep relationships goes beyond one's own social circle. A further layer of community spirit can be provided by interacting with neighbors. Plan a neighborhood get-together where everyone can share decorations or holiday refreshments. Developing ties with the local population promotes a feeling of security and inclusion. People can improve each other's lives by joining together to form a network of support.

Strong relationships can result from embracing variety in holiday celebrations. Everyone's experience is enhanced when customs from other cultures are accepted. Putting together a multicultural event fosters admiration and understanding by educating attendees about one another's traditions. Sharing distinctive customs, such as a holiday tale, a special meal, or music, weaves a beautiful tapestry of experiences that honor difference while promoting togetherness.

Keeping in touch is aided by technology, particularly in this increasingly digital age. Family members who reside far away can take part in celebrations thanks to virtual get-togethers. For those who are unable to attend in person, a video call during a holiday meal can provide joy and humor. Sharing Christmas moments on social media can inspire friends and family to get together and enjoy, especially if they live far away.

Deeper connections are also fostered by being in the present. It's simple to lose sight of what really matters in the thick of the stress of event planning and gift purchasing. During gatherings, encourage everyone to turn off their devices so that genuine conversations and shared experiences can take place. Present-moment mindfulness fosters real connections where everyone is respected, heard, and feels valued.

Establishing goals centered on deep connections can improve the entire experience as the holidays progress. Think on the most important relationships in your life and give them top priority. Be open-minded and prepared to welcome the opportunities that present themselves as the season progresses. Every encounter turns into a chance to spread happiness, love, and laughter.

Establishing a welcoming atmosphere is essential to building relationships. The ambiance should exude acceptance and friendliness, whether you're throwing an open house or inviting friends over for a relaxed get-together. Meaningful encounters are facilitated by small details like festive décor and comfortable seating. Encourage visitors to tell their tales in order to foster an inclusive atmosphere where all opinions are valued.

Adding a lighthearted element to the holiday season can improve relationships and lighten the mood. Take part in enjoyable activities; karaoke nights, board games, and holiday crafts may all spark friendship and laughter. People form bonds over happy times and create enduring, happy memories when they share them.

Lastly, thinking back on the relationships formed throughout the season might help you identify what really counts. After the Christmas celebrations are over, pause to reflect on the joy and relationships that have been cultivated. Express your gratitude to the people who helped make the season memorable by sending sincere letters, giving them small gifts, or just spending time with them. A more satisfying holiday season and the basis for enduring relationships might result from acknowledging these ties.

The holidays serve as a reminder of the value of connection in a world full of distractions. Families and communities can make this time of year a celebration of joy, love, and unity by seizing the chance to engage in meaningful connections.

Bonds are forged during every time spent together, forming a rich tapestry of shared memories that endure long after the decorations are taken down. By highlighting these ties, the holiday season becomes a treasured occasion that speaks to our innermost feelings.

Cultivating Family Bonds

As everyone gathers around the table, laughter erupts, the aroma of freshly baked cookies permeates the air, and the happiness of being together casts a nice blanket of warmth around the space. The art of creating family ties through shared activities throughout the holidays elevates everyday events into remarkable recollections. Adopting activities that appeal to all members of the family can help create a rich tapestry of love and togetherness as families look for methods to deepen their bonds.

Baking and cooking are ageless customs that bring family members into the kitchen together. Consider making a batch of your favorite Christmas cookies, in which everyone contributes. While older siblings measure out ingredients, younger siblings can decorate with colorful sprinkles. This exercise not only encourages creativity but also imparts valuable life lessons. The laughs and conversation that were exchanged during the procedure are carried with every taste of those delicious pastries. A sensory experience that lasts long after the last cookie is eaten is produced by flooding the senses with mouthwatering flavors and scents.

Creating seasonal décor can help foster a sense of community. Encourage everyone to let their creativity run wild by setting up a craft station with glitter, glue, paper, and scissors. Each ornament can tell a narrative about how it was made and end up being a family heirloom. Family ties are strengthened as thoughts and conversations flow together. These handcrafted decorations not only give the house a unique touch, but they also perfectly capture the love and teamwork that characterize the season.

Another approach to foster relationships is through family game nights. An regular evening can be turned into an exciting experience by playing card games, board games, or even trivia challenges. Cheers, laughing, and occasionally lighthearted banter are sparked by the excitement of friendly rivalry. These times build friendships and produce internal jokes that turn into treasured memories. These game nights can develop into cherished customs that are looked forward to year after year as the Christmas season goes on.

An exciting energy that can strengthen family ties is brought about by outdoor activities. The crisp air and laughter enhance the delight of the season, whether it is spent ice skating, sledding, or creating a snowman. Everyone can relax and be reminded that the purpose of the holidays is to enjoy one other by participating in physical activities. Unexpected discoveries—a fallen pinecone, a rare bird, or a stunning winter scene—can come from even a basic nature stroll, deepening family bonds.

During the holidays, volunteering is a great way to share kindness and build relationships. Get the family involved in community service by volunteering at a charity event or giving food to a nearby shelter. These common experiences foster compassion and empathy, establishing morals that are applicable much beyond the holidays. Making a difference together creates enduring memories focused on giving back and strengthens a sense of purpose and connection.

Making a holiday book for the family may be a rewarding endeavor. Gather images, anecdotes, and recollections from previous festivities to create a narrative that encapsulates your family's customs. This common pastime strengthens bonds and emphasizes the love that permeates every holiday when you get together to remember special times. The experience is both fun and important because it makes you laugh and feel nostalgic every time you flip the page.

The holiday season is made more magical by incorporating themed movie evenings. For a comfortable movie night, pick some beloved Christmas movies, crack open some popcorn, and curl up with blankets. Heartfelt conversations about the films' themes and how they speak to your family might result from these shared viewing experiences. The delight of following cherished characters on their adventures turns into a ritual of bonding that strengthens bonds and fosters common interests.

Creating a gratitude jar with your family will help them feel more grateful throughout the holidays. Throughout December, give out slips of paper so that everyone can jot down their blessings and put them to the jar. Get everyone together and read each message out loud on a selected evening. By reminding everyone of the love and benefits in their lives, this easy yet powerful exercise fosters a sense of connectedness and thankfulness.

ENCHANTED NOEL: SANTA'S GUIDE TO A PERFECT HOLIDAY

Having storytelling evenings might help foster closer ties. Every member of the family takes turns telling stories, whether they are from their personal experiences or their favorite fairy tales. Everyone opens up to share experiences and dreams during these sessions, which encourage candor, laughter, and occasionally even tears. Family bonds are strengthened and a sense of belonging is created by the warmth of shared memories.

Think about planning a family photo session to document unscripted moments all season long. These pictures turn become treasures whether you hire an expert or set up a do-it-yourself station with festive backdrops and decorations. Every photo captures a different aspect of your family's story, capturing the pleasure and laughter that were shared throughout the holidays. These pictures will remind you of the relationships formed during this unique period when you look back on them throughout time.

A greater understanding of one another can be achieved by scheduling time for each family member to express their Christmas goals and wishes. Set aside a comfortable evening when everyone may share their hopes for the upcoming season. An atmosphere of love and support is created when family members listen to one another's goals, highlighting the importance of each person's emotions and ambitions.

It might be exciting and joyful to go on a holiday excursion together, like going to a nearby tree farm or shopping at seasonal markets. These excursions offer chances for discovery, amusement, and camaraderie, resulting in memories that are frequently recounted at subsequent events. The excitement of choosing the ideal tree or discovering unusual presents gives a sense of adventure that fortifies relationships via shared experiences.

As the holidays approach, incorporating family-bonding activities into the schedule fosters a festive mood that permeates the entire house. Families will treasure these moments for years to come since they are full of love, laughter, and creativity. As families participate in a variety of activities, creating experiences that strengthen their ties and bring them joy, the spirit of connection is evident.

Spreading Kindness and Cheer

A remarkable reminder of the strength of community and generosity is provided by the holiday season. This time of year, when happiness is abundant, offers a special chance to promote cheer and goodwill. Little acts of kindness may make a big difference and spread happiness throughout communities, schools, and local organizations. These deeds of compassion create a fabric of connection that draws people closer together, which is what makes the season so beautiful.

To encourage relationships among neighbors, think about holding a community event. People are encouraged to get together, share recipes, and spend time together through a casual potluck or cookie exchange. To allow for the blending of many cuisines and tales, invite everyone to provide a food that reflects their ethnicity. This celebration of culinary innovation breaks down boundaries that may exist in communal life while igniting discussions and fostering friendships.

A communal giving spirit might be sparked by planning a toy drive. Collaborate with neighborhood groups or educational institutions to gather brand-new or lightly used toys for underprivileged kids. Place collection containers in easily accessible areas so that families may easily contribute. Use local posters and social media to spread the word about the drive and highlight the happiness that comes from helping others. Throughout the season, there is a touching mood created by seeing the community come together to collect toys for underprivileged children.

Sharing food with people experiencing food insecurity is another powerful concept. Plan a community lunch or food pantry event in conjunction with your neighborhood food banks. To ensure that people and families in need experience the warmth of the season, get together with friends and family to cook dinners or put together food hampers. In addition to satisfying hungry stomachs, this deed of kindness uplifts people's emotions and serves as a reminder that nobody should have to go without over the holidays.

During this unique moment, volunteering in community centers or shelters is a direct method to make a difference in people's lives. Help with Christmas activities, including throwing kid-friendly parties or feeding families, is greatly appreciated by many groups. Helping with holiday crafts or serving food on Christmas Day can make people happy and help them make treasured memories. By connecting with those in need, this activity turns the holiday into a time of warmth and kindness for everyone.

During the holidays, the power of cards can also be quite effective. Get family and friends together to make handmade cards with meaningful messages for elderly people in the area or those residing in assisted living facilities. Just sending a card can improve people's emotions and fight loneliness, which tends to worsen over the holidays. Writing these cards turns into a lovely opportunity to connect and show gratitude, letting everyone know they are loved and taken care of.

By interacting with nearby schools, we may spread the generosity to the next generation. Students are encouraged to enjoy the joy of giving by planning a service activity with a holiday theme, such as writing letters to veterans serving overseas or assembling care packages for classmates in need. Children develop a sense of responsibility and connection when teachers and students work together to integrate conversations about compassion and community service into curricula. Children who participate in service projects develop lifelong values.

Organize a holiday market to promote local small businesses and artists while bringing joy to the community. In order to transform the event into a celebration of local ingenuity, invite local vendors to display their goods, services, and crafts. With the help of music, decorations, and kid-friendly activities, create a joyous mood. Urge everyone to shop locally, emphasizing the value of helping small businesses and uniting the neighborhood in a festive celebration.

Participating in neighborhood clean-up days can boost pride and a sense of accomplishment. Organize your neighbors and friends to pick up trash in the parks or on the streets. During the holidays, community beautification fosters a sense of pride and responsibility for common areas. The mere act of uniting around a shared objective turns routine chores into unforgettable moments full of friendship and laughter

Caroling during the holidays can be a fun way to spread happiness. Get your loved ones together and form a joyful group, going out into the neighborhood to sing traditional Christmas tunes. Singing at neighborhood hospitals, assisted living facilities, or community centers cheers up people who might otherwise feel lonely throughout the season. People of all ages and backgrounds can connect via the power of music, which uplifts everyone's spirits and spreads joy.

Putting together gift-making workshops for the community can encourage creativity and camaraderie. Organize a do-it-yourself event where attendees make their own wreaths, ornaments, and other decorations. Give everyone the tools and direction they need to express their creative side while connecting over common experiences. In addition to providing one-of-a-kind presents that include memories and personal tales, the process of creating together promotes a sense of community.

A rich tapestry of cultural interchange is produced when the community is invited to share their holiday customs through storytelling. Organize a gathering where people can exchange stories, recipes, and customs. By reminding everyone that every story adds to the Christmas spirit, this event fosters a respect and knowledge of the community's many customs. It helps participants feel united and like they belong.

Supporting neighborhood nonprofits encourages people to give more during the holidays. Urge your friends and neighbors to volunteer or make donations to local groups. Emphasize the value of helping those who put in endless effort to improve the community. This group effort fosters a culture of compassion that goes far beyond the holidays and elevates the festive spirit.

Making a holiday newsletter for the community can be a fun way to keep everyone updated and involved. Emphasize neighborhood-wide activities, events, and deeds of community service. Residents should be encouraged to contribute by sharing their stories of kindness and hard work. This newsletter turns into a celebration of community spirit, encouraging others to join the continuous path of connection and kindness.

The holiday season becomes a tapestry of compassion and camaraderie as each act of kindness adds to a greater movement of joy and generosity. Adopting these concepts and projects fosters a sense of community and belonging while establishing an atmosphere in which everyone can prosper. Every act, no matter

ENCHANTED NOEL: SANTA'S GUIDE TO A PERFECT HOLIDAY

how small, during this season of giving is essential to creating a community full of love, generosity, and memories that will be treasured for years to come.

Chapter 6
Reflecting and Recharging

THERE IS A MIXTURE of excitement and fatigue as the last days of the holiday season draw near. Once glistening with excitement, the lights now remind us of hectic days, late nights, and the frenetic festivities. Like a warm fire calling you to rest, the need for introspection and rejuvenation arises amid the chaos. In order for the memories and experiences to get ingrained in your heart, this chapter encourages you to take a moment to stop, take a deep breath, and enjoy the season that has come to pass.

Find a peaceful area to start, maybe with a hot blanket and a steaming mug of your preferred libation. This is a sacred time to connect with yourself, not to rush to the next duty. Take out a notepad or journal and write down your views regarding the holidays. What were the happy moments? Which customs struck a strong chord with you? By weaving a story of your experiences, this technique helps you create a tapestry of memories that you may look back on in the future.

Think about the warmth of a friend's embrace during a Christmas get-together, the joy in a child's eyes as they unwrap presents, or the laughter shared around the dinner table. In addition to being enjoyable, thinking back on these encounters strengthens the bonds that are really important. It's simple to lose sight of the beauty of these little but significant moments in the middle of hectic days. By giving them deliberate attention, you let their importance become clear to you and build a positive energy bank that you may use long after the decorations are taken down.

Consider the difficulties encountered during the season as you reflect. Why did it feel so overwhelming? Did you have any stressful or disappointing moments? Recognizing these emotions is crucial because it enables you to determine what may need to be changed for the upcoming year. Did you feel frazzled after purchasing at the last minute? Maybe next year we should make a more formal plan. Perhaps a certain family custom didn't appeal to everyone. By making a note of these experiences, you can intentionally mold the future and transform obstacles into teaching moments.

An important part of this process is the power of appreciation. During the holidays, make it a habit to write down your blessings. Expressing thankfulness helps you turn your attention from what might have gone wrong to the wealth of goodness all around you, whether it's the warmth of family gathered together, the generosity of a stranger, or a thoughtful gift. This small yet meaningful deed can elevate your spirits and make you feel happy and warm within.

After you've had time to contemplate, think about strategies to rejuvenate yourself. We frequently put a lot of emotional, physical, and mental strain on ourselves over the holiday season. Making time for oneself becomes crucial. This isn't always about lavish spa treatments or extravagant displays; sometimes it's about doing tiny things for yourself. Take a long bath, light a candle, or curl up with a nice book. Make time for things that feed your spirit and provide you a much-needed break from the busy celebrations.

Making a connection with nature can also be a very effective approach to rejuvenate. You can clear your head and rejuvenate your mind with a vigorous walk in the cool winter air. Experience the chill of a winter air on your face or the crunch of snow under your boots. Nature has the special capacity to bring us back to earth by serving as a reminder of the beauty of the here and now as well as life's small joys. These encounters can help you declutter your mind and start the new year with a new outlook.

During this time of reflection, think about contacting loved ones. Discuss your ideas, observations, and takeaways from the holidays. Discussions can strengthen bonds and yield surprising discoveries. Sharing a cup of tea and talking about holiday experiences can occasionally foster a feeling of camaraderie and belonging that uplifts the soul.

Another great way to recharge is through creative expression. Take part in activities that let you express your feelings and ideas, such as writing, drawing, or making. Allowing your imagination to flow can be quite therapeutic and aid in the processing of experiences. Making artwork with a Christmas theme or writing letters to loved ones to show your gratitude and affection may bring you delight. This relationship between introspection and creativity helps you comprehend your experiences more deeply and incorporates them into a more comprehensive story.

Think about establishing goals for the upcoming year as you rejuvenate. Making resolutions that are void by February is not the point here. It's about adopting an attitude that embraces development and optimism. What do you hope to remember from this year's holidays? Maybe it's the joy in small things, the value of connection, or the giving spirit. By directing your behaviors and choices for the upcoming year, setting intentions helps you develop a feeling of purpose.

Remember that the holidays are a reminder of what really counts during this time of introspection and rejuvenation. The relationships we cultivate, the experiences we make, and the love we share are what really matter amid the glitter and excitement. By accepting this insight, you may give your daily existence purpose and let the magic of the season last long after the holidays are over.

Spend a time appreciating your trip, including the love, laughter, chaos, and serenity. Every event adds to the intricate fabric of your life, weaving a tale that keeps getting told. The beauty of this season is etched in your heart, ready to evoke happiness and camaraderie in the months ahead, even after the decorations are taken down and the holiday bustle fades.

A deeper connection to oneself and the season is made possible by the practice of reflecting and recharging amid the rush of events and festivities. By embracing this moment of reflection, one can cultivate appreciation, joy, and clarity, turning what could otherwise seem like a short vacation into a treasured chapter in one's life. The holiday spirit endures and shapes our intentional and loving approach to every day.

Post-Holiday Check-In

The final traces of Christmas spirit are still present in the air after the celebrations have subsided. Families are invited to reflect on their recent celebrations as the decorations come down and the last of the gingerbread cookies disappear. Everyone may evaluate what really made people happy, what didn't work, and how to create a more captivating experience the next time by embracing the post-holiday check-in.

Getting together around the table is a great place to start. Bring all of the family members who took part in the celebrations together, including the children, spouses, and relatives. This is an opportunity to appreciate the positive moments and draw lessons from the less-than-ideal ones, not to point fingers or place blame. Exchange anecdotes, giggles, and even embarrassing situations that become inside jokes. This candid discussion promotes connection and candid input regarding the things that really struck a chord over the holidays.

Think about delving into the particulars of what made each occasion special. Which activities made people grin the most? Was it the frantic gift-wrapping party, the marathon of holiday movies, or the baking sessions? Make a list of these highlights and note any recurring themes. Maybe it was the excitement of attempting a new custom, or perhaps it was the delight of spending time together that struck out. Documenting these experiences might provide as a wealth of ideas for the upcoming year.

Then turn your attention to what seemed overwhelming. Talk about the chores that made you feel stressed or exhausted. Did the shopping turn into a last-minute flurry? Were too many events planned in close succession? The first step in making future experiences more seamless is recognizing these pain areas. Families can come up with solutions together when problems are openly discussed, which makes the following holiday more pleasurable.

A more thorough examination of the budget is also informative. Was spending in line with projections? Determine whether the money spent improved the experience or caused regrets. Expensive presents could have been intended to impress, but they instead caused tension. Think about putting more emphasis on experiences than material presents. A sentimental card or a handcrafted present frequently has greater significance than the newest technology. Make a list of inexpensive, enjoyable ideas, such as a basic craft activity or a neighborhood potluck.

Traditions have an important role in this assessment as well. Which ones have a strong sense of significance? Were there any that were changeable or perhaps interchangeable? While certain customs may seem forced and depressing, others may strike a deep chord, fostering a sense of continuity and community. A more satisfying vacation experience can result from considering which customs were friendly and which seemed like a job. Be open to trying out novel concepts that could enhance the holiday experience, such as introducing new games or investigating various cuisines.

Making a plan for the upcoming year is an exciting next step after analyzing what worked and what didn't. Write down any thoughts sparked by this check-in procedure. Maybe that means streamlining meal preparation, adopting a minimalist approach to décor, or starting sooner to prevent the Christmas rush. This is more than simply a list of things to do; it's a collection of concepts that are brimming with creativity and community, poised to blossom into something truly remarkable.

Making a holiday notebook or shared document might be a useful tool for preparing in the future. Throughout the year, invite everyone to share their ideas, opinions, and suggestions. This continuous cooperation ensures that everyone's opinions are acknowledged and keeps the festive spirit alive. Any time an idea comes to mind, it can be incorporated into the group holiday plan, whether it's a humorous new custom or an enjoyable pastime.

A crucial component of this introspection is making self-care a priority as the post-holiday blues set in. Burnout can be avoided and the soul can be revitalized by taking time for oneself. Ask each member of the household to list the things that help them relax. Prioritizing well-being becomes crucial, whether it is through engaging in a pastime, taking a nature walk, or curling up with a beloved

ENCHANTED NOEL: SANTA'S GUIDE TO A PERFECT HOLIDAY

book. The foundation for a better and healthier attitude to upcoming holidays is laid by this emphasis on self-care.

In this assessment, talking about the value of connection and community is equally crucial. During the holidays, were there chances to interact and get to know your neighbors or friends? Consider how your personal celebrations were enhanced by showing kindness to others. Organizing a charity drive or working at a nearby shelter can turn the Christmas enthusiasm into a shared experience that benefits everyone. Maybe it's time to look for new ways to give back to the community.

Creating an atmosphere of thankfulness offers a useful prism through which to assess the holiday season. Every member of the family can express their gratitude for the previous season. In addition to strengthening emotional ties, these reflections assist everyone in concentrating on the celebration's good elements. Throughout the year, everyone can donate to a gratitude jar, which could help establish gratitude as a regular practice.

Finally, once the chaos of the holidays subsides, promote an attitude of adaptability. Plans occasionally take a detour because life happens. Joy and flexibility are fostered by acknowledging that the unexpected can result in memorable experiences. The impromptu memories made during the holiday season are frequently what make it so lovely.

The post-holiday check-in evolves from a simple assessment into a deep dialogue that fortifies family ties and prepares the ground for subsequent festivities. Families may create a holiday experience that truly connects each year by accepting the lessons learnt and concentrating on what truly makes people happy. The upcoming season promises to be an adventure full of warmth, fun, and treasured memories thanks to introspection, planning, and creativity.

Self-Care in the Festive Season

The holiday season, with its sparkling lights and the cozy smell of freshly made cookies, can sometimes feel like a double-edged blade. The joy of celebrations, family get-togethers, and the giving spirit are on the one hand. However, even the most passionate holiday enthusiast may feel exhausted and overburdened by the pressure to plan the ideal event. Making well-being a priority during this busy period turns the turmoil into a loving experience.

In the middle of the holiday rush, scheduling time for self-care doesn't mean compromising happiness; rather, it means embracing it. Finding methods to fit relaxation into a hectic schedule can help you feel more energized and upbeat, making celebrations joyous rather than stressful. Finding brief periods of time during the day to concentrate on one's own well-being is a straightforward strategy. It could be as short as taking a few deep breaths, drinking tea in a peaceful corner, or even sneaking away for a quick stroll in the cool winter air. These times establish a haven where the body and mind can rest.

Developing a well-rounded holiday itinerary is crucial to preserving wellbeing. Managing social gatherings, career commitments, and family responsibilities can easily become an onerous juggling act. Making time for oneself can turn stress into harmony, even though a calendar full of events may seem joyous. Allow for unplanned time when organizing your schedule; a Sunday afternoon free of obligations can be used for a relaxing family movie marathon or just to relax.

Setting limits is also advantageous during this exciting time of year. Overcommitting is frequently the result of the desire to please everyone. Prioritizing personal needs while managing expectations can be achieved by politely refusing invites or offering other plans. This harmony keeps self-care at the forefront while enabling sincere relationships with loved ones. In the midst of the chaos, it's perfectly appropriate to take a break and catch your breath.

ENCHANTED NOEL: SANTA'S GUIDE TO A PERFECT HOLIDAY

One of the most effective ways to combat Christmas stress is to find joy in the little things. Accept the small things that make you happy and comfortable. Enjoy a favorite seasonal food, light a candle, or take up a relaxing pastime. These small pleasures, like making your own ornaments, reading by the fireplace, or taking a long bath, provide a calming environment in the middle of the chaos. Gratitude and satisfaction are made possible by being in the present rather than rushing through these times.

Holiday routines can incorporate mindfulness exercises easily, providing a break from the mayhem. In the midst of the chaos, one might ground themselves using breathing techniques, meditation, or mild yoga. Think about taking a few deliberate breaths at the beginning of each day to help the mind relax before beginning the day's activities. The holiday spirit can thrive rather than wane when even a short moment is taken to recognize ideas and sentiments.

Overshadowed by decadent feasts and sweet desserts, nutrition frequently suffers during the holidays. Making nutrition a priority may energize the body and mind. Balance the festive treats with nutritious options by preparing hearty meals that are bursting with seasonal fruits and vegetables. It's easy to get caught up in the hustle and forget to drink enough water. Having a water bottle close at hand acts as a reminder to hydrate and fuel the body.

During this time of year, physical activity becomes essential to preserving wellbeing. Elevating mood and energy levels can be achieved by ice skating, a lively stroll around the neighborhood, or even a dance party in the living room. Endorphins are released when the body moves, which naturally reduces stress and anxiety. By involving loved ones in these activities, you can make working out a joyful family activity that builds memories and promotes a healthy habit.

Don't be afraid to ask friends and family for help as the season goes on. A sense of belonging and community is fostered by sharing emotions and experiences. Leaning on loved ones can ease pressures, whether it's offering sanity-maintenance advice or screaming about Christmas stress. Putting together get-togethers that emphasize connection, like a potluck supper where everyone contributes their favorite dish, promotes camaraderie and laughing and builds a network of support among the chaos.

Accepting creativity also provides a way to take care of oneself. It can be helpful to try new dishes, decorate the house, or do arts and crafts. These pursuits offer a creative outlet that facilitates stress reduction and self-expression.

Organize a crafting session with loved ones to make it a happy occasion that also serves as quality time spent together.

A more tranquil experience may result from limiting exposure to seasonal stressors, such as crowded malls or excessive screen time. To avoid feeling pressured, choose to purchase online or go to local markets at slower times. A media diet that emphasizes upbeat Christmas films or music fosters a joyful rather than stressful environment. These minor adjustments make the holidays more joyful and well-balanced.

During this hectic period, practicing thankfulness can also help you see things differently. A positive outlook can be developed by thinking back on happy times, giving thanks, or even keeping a gratitude diary. Express gratitude to family members by writing little notes of praise and leaving them all throughout the house. This creates a loving and appreciative environment. By encouraging everyone to appreciate the beauty of the season, this easy activity improves wellbeing and connections.

Adding playful moments during the holiday season can encourage happiness and good humor. With family and friends, games, crafts, or outdoor activities foster fun and laughter. Selecting activities that everyone enjoys will help to create a welcoming environment that promotes communication and camaraderie. A family baking competition or a game night with holiday-themed trivia unites everyone in a lighthearted manner and serves as a reminder of the happiness that comes from connection.

It's critical to recognize the emotional toll that the holidays may take. Anxiety or loneliness might set in, especially for people who are separated from loved ones. It's critical to acknowledge these feelings and make room for them. Think about contacting friends or family for a conversation, or maybe volunteering in the neighborhood to meet people who might have similar emotions. Accepting the reality of emotions during this time of year builds strength and resilience, fostering a supportive atmosphere for all.

Taking care of oneself and one's wellbeing is essential to creating a happy holiday experience. Every movement, from fun exchanges to moments of mindfulness, adds to the cozy and connected ambiance. Making time for rest and connection in the middle of the chaos turns the holidays into a period of renewal, resulting in treasured moments and enduring memories with loved ones. The

ENCHANTED NOEL: SANTA'S GUIDE TO A PERFECT HOLIDAY

holiday spirit shines brightly for everyone as the festive season transforms into a celebration of happiness, connection, and wellbeing.